THE STORY OF SALT

Published in paperback in Great Britain in
2019 by Wayland
© Hodder and Stoughton, 2016

All rights reserved.

Written by Alex Woolf
Cover illustration by Donough O'Malley

Editor: Julia Adams
Designer: Paper Wasp Books

ISBN: 978 0 7502 9981 7

10 9 8 7 6 5 4 3 2 1

Wayland
An imprint of
Hachette Children's Books
Part of Hodder & Stoughton
Carmelite House
50 Victoria Embankment
London, EC4Y 0DZ

An Hachette UK Company
www.hachette.co.uk
www.hachettechildrens.co.uk

Printed in China

Picture credits: p4 © Foodfolio/the food passionates/Corbis; p6 © Food Photo & Video/the food passionates/Corbis; p7 © Ina Peters/Westend61/Corbis (t); p7 © perschfoto/dpa/Corbis (m); p7 © the food passionates/Corbis (b); p8 © Freddie Parkinson/Demotix/Corbis; p9 © Guillaume Horcajuelo/epa/Corbis (t); p9 © STR/epa/Corbis (b); p10 © Oxford Science Archive/Print Collector/Getty Images; p11 © Popperfoto/Getty Images; p12 © The Image Works/TopFoto; p13 © Reza/Webistan/Corbis; p14 © Stocktrek Images/Stocktrek Images/Corbis; p15 © Lisovskaya Natalia/The Picture Pantry/Corbis; p16 © Leemage/UIG/Getty Images; p17 © TOSHIFUMI KITAMURA/AFP/Getty Images; p18 © The Granger Collection/ TopFoto; p19 © Uwe Kraft/imageBROKER/Corbis; p20 © Howard Sayer/Shutterstock; p21 © FPG/Getty Images (t); p21 © Witold Skrypczak/Lonely Planet Images/Getty Images (b); p23 © World History Archive/ TopFoto; p23 © Chris Howes/Wild Places Photography/Alamy Stock Photo; p24 © Bygone Collection/Alamy Stock Photo; p25 © Corbis; p26 © Hulton Archive/Getty Images; p27 © Hulton Archive/Getty Images; p28 © OMER SALEEM/epa/Corbis p29; © Diego Giudice/Corbis. Background images and other graphic elements courtesy of Shutterstock.com.

Every effort has been made to clear copyright. Should there be any inadvertent omission, please apply to the publisher for rectification.

The website addresses (URLs) included in this book were valid at the time of going to press However, it is possible that contents or addresses may have changed since the publication of this book. No responsibility for any such changes can be accepted by either the author or the Publisher.

CONTENTS

WHAT IS SALT?	4
SALT FOR SEASONING	6
HOW IS SALT PRODUCED?	8
SALT FOR PRESERVING FOOD	10
SALT IN THE ANCIENT WORLD	12
SALT AND OUR HEALTH	14
SALT IN RELIGION	16
SALT IN THE MIDDLE AGES	18
EXPLORING THE NEW WORLD	20
SALT WARS	22
SALT IN EARLY AMERICA	24
THE SALT MARCH	26
SALT IN TODAY'S WORLD	28
TIMELINE	30
GLOSSARY	31
INDEX	32

WHAT IS SALT?

We usually find it sitting next to the pepper on the dining table. It has a very simple appearance: tiny white grains that we sprinkle on our food. And its flavour is so familiar. We often think of it as the opposite of sweet. It tastes great on chips, peanuts and popcorn. But what exactly *is* salt? Where does it come from? And why do we use it more than any other condiment? In this book, we'll explore the answers to these questions, and along the way we'll learn some sensational secrets about salt.

THE TASTY MINERAL

Salt is a mineral – a solid substance that is found in nature. It takes the form of white, cube-shaped crystals that smell of nothing, and taste… well, salty! Salt is made up of two elements, 'sodium' (40 per cent) and 'chlorine' (60 per cent), which together form the chemical compound 'sodium chloride'. So if you ever hear anyone mention sodium chloride, they're actually talking about salt! The flavour we know as salt comes from the sodium, which belongs to a group of chemicals called 'alkali' metals. Other chemicals in this group, such as 'lithium' and 'potassium', have a similar salty taste.

Salt is essential for human and animal life. The flavour of salt is one of the basic human tastes.

WHERE IS IT FOUND?

Salt is found in the Earth in a form known as rock salt. There are also vast quantities in the seas, oceans, and saltwater lakes. There is even salt in us, as there is in all animals and, to a lesser extent, plants. It's in our tissues and bodily fluids, which is why tears taste salty. Our bodies need salt to function. Yet the body can't produce salt by itself, so we need to get it from food.

HOW IS SALT FORMED?

Salt forms when atoms of sodium (Na) and chlorine (Cl) react together. The atoms, in this case, are known as 'ions'. Ions are atoms that have lost or gained electrons in their outer shells so they carry an electric charge. Sodium ions have lost an electron so they have a positive charge. Chloride ions have gained an electron so they have a negative charge. In the world of ions, opposites attract, so they come together to form sodium chloride (NaCl), which is salt. This diagram shows how a sodium atom (Na) becomes a positively charged sodium ion (Na+) when it loses an electron to a chlorine atom. The chlorine atom (Cl), by gaining the electron, becomes a negatively charged chloride ion (Cl-). The oppositely charged ions then attract each other to form sodium chloride (NaCl).

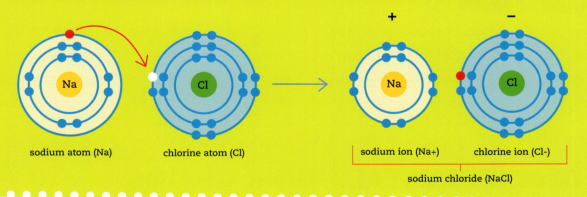

sodium atom (Na)   chlorine atom (Cl)   sodium ion (Na+)   chlorine ion (Cl-)

sodium chloride (NaCl)

AN AMAZING HISTORY

Salt has a long and fascinating history. For thousands of years we've used it to add flavour to food, and also to preserve food. Before refrigeration, meat and fish had to be salted to stop them from going bad. Salt has played an essential role since the dawn of human history.

The quest for this simple substance has driven trade and exploration. It's built cities, destroyed kingdoms, and started wars and revolutions. It's even formed the basis for religious rituals. One way or another, salt has helped shape our world.

Salt for Seasoning

Salt is the oldest and most widely used food seasoning, and its flavour is one of the basic tastes that the human tongue can identify. Other such tastes include sweetness, sourness and bitterness. We use salt in cooking to add flavour to food that might otherwise taste bland. We also keep it in a salt cellar on the dining table for those who want to add salt to food that has already been served.

The Joy of Salt

We love the taste of salt because our bodies need it. It is one of the most powerful tools a cook has for improving the flavour of food. But, like all good things, we shouldn't overdo it.

Salt shouldn't drown out the flavour of food or try to replace it. Salt should enhance and intensify flavours. For best results, it's generally better to add salt late in the cooking process.

Black Crystals, Pink Grains

In India, people make black salt by mixing saltwater with seeds from the harad fruit. The mixture is left to evaporate, leaving a residue of black salt crystals. When the crystals are ground, the resulting powder is pink. Indians call this salt *kala namak*.

DIFFERENT KINDS

There are many different kinds of salt. The crystals can be fine- or coarse-grained, flaky or even spherical. Salt isn't always white either. It can be blue, green, black, grey, silver, pink, red, orange or purple. There are, however, three basic categories of salt, as follows:

Sea salt is produced through the evaporation of ocean water or water from saltwater lakes. There is little processing, so it contains trace minerals, which vary depending on the water source. Some gourmets (food experts) claim that sea salt tastes better than table salt and gives additional flavour to foods. It certainly feels different in the mouth, having a coarser texture, and the mineral content may affect the taste. Like table salt, it contains around 40 per cent sodium.

Table salt is the most common type of salt used for seasoning. It is mined from salt deposits and is usually ground to a fine texture to make it easier to mix with food. Traces of minerals such as calcium, copper, magnesium and iron are removed as these can spoil the flavour or reduce the nutritional content of food. Anti-caking agents are added to make the salt more free-flowing. Some table salt contains iodine as a health supplement.

Kosher salt is so-called because it's used to make meat kosher (fit for consumption according to Jewish food laws) by drawing out and removing the blood from the meat's surface. Kosher salt has larger grains than table salt, and the cubic salt crystals are flattened under pressure into a plate-like shape.

FLAVOURED SALTS

Some salts are seasoned with herbs, such as onion, hickory or garlic, to add extra subtle flavours to food. Lime-flavoured sea salt, for example, is recommended for fish. There are even sweetened salts that are, delicious on cheesecake and ice cream!

HOW IS SALT PRODUCED?

Salt is in the ground and it's in the world's oceans, seas and saltwater lakes. There are three main methods of extracting it. One is to dig it out of the earth by deep-shaft mining. The second, called solar evaporation, is to allow saltwater to evaporate in the sun in shallow ponds, leaving the salt behind. The third, called solution mining, involves injecting water into salt deposits and then evaporating the resulting saltwater.

DEEP-SHAFT MINING

Salt was deposited millions of years ago when much of the Earth was covered by sea. The deposits may be found in veins, like coal, or in domes that formed when pressures inside the Earth forced salt up through cracks in the rock. In deep-shaft mining, shafts are sunk into the salt bed, then 'rooms' are cut into the salt layer. The rooms are cut in a checkerboard pattern, leaving solid areas to give support to the mine roof. Usually, 45–65 per cent of the salt is removed. Once removed, the salt is crushed and then transported to the surface.

A deep-shaft rock salt mine in Carrickfergus, Northern Ireland.

SOLAR EVAPORATION

This is the oldest method of salt production, used in countries with warm climates and regular coastal winds. Saltwater from lakes or seas is captured in shallow ponds that are exposed to the sun and wind. As the water evaporates and becomes more concentrated with salt, it is moved along a chain of ponds. When it starts to crystallise, it can be harvested. At the harvesting plant, it's washed to remove impurities, then drained, before final processing.

A worker collects fleur de sel, a hand-harvested sea salt, in France.

A worker boils brine to make salt in Zigong, Sichuan province, China.

SOLUTION MINING

With this method, two wells are drilled into the salt deposit, connected by a tunnel. Water is pumped down one well, dissolving the salt below. The resulting 'brine' is forced to the surface through the other well. Once purified, the brine is pumped into a series of closed vessels. The vessels are heated, causing water to evaporate and salt crystals to grow. The mixture of brine and crystals flows from chamber to chamber. The remaining salt is spun to remove any moisture.

HAND HARVESTING

In some countries, including Spain, Greece, Canada and Mexico, sea salt is still produced without machines. Among the most famous hand-harvested salts is *fleur de sel* ('flower of salt'), from Guérande in northern France. In a tradition that goes back to 868 CE, seawater is guided into shallow marshes where it evaporates. Women known as *paludiers* then use rakes to delicately remove a fine layer of salt from the surface. Fleur de sel is sprinkled on food prior to eating. It is never used in cooking.

SALT FOR PRESERVING FOOD

Salt isn't used only to flavour food, but also to preserve it. Before the invention of refrigeration in the 19th century, salting, or 'salt-curing' (preserving food in dry salt) and 'pickling' (preserving food in brine) were among the only ways of preventing food from going bad. Today we still use salt-curing, for example with ham, bacon, corned beef and pastrami. We pickle tuna, herring and anchovies, and vegetables like cabbage, gherkins and onions.

SALT-CURING

The ancient Egyptians may have been the first people to realise that salt could be used to preserve foods. And they didn't just use it to stop meat from going off – mummies were preserved with salt, too!

Historically, meat was cut into slabs and laid like bricks in a keg, or wooden barrel. No two pieces touched each other and salt was packed in the spaces between. This was how meat was preserved, for example, during long sea voyages.

Traditionally, meat was 'dry-cured', which can take months. Dry-curing was done in cold weather so meat wouldn't spoil while the salt was taking effect.

Dry-curing of meat or fish can take several months.

An assembly line of women at a pickling plant in the early 20th century.

PICKLING

This process was once used for preserving all kinds of food. Today it is mostly used for fish and vegetables. Pickling makes use of the preservative qualities of both salt and an 'acid', such as vinegar. To make pickles, sea salt and vinegar are added to water, along with other ingredients such as sugar and herbs. The mixture is then heated and stirred until the salt dissolves. The solution is poured into a sealable jar, over the food that is being preserved.

DID YOU KNOW?

In the 19th century it was discovered that if salt is mixed with a chemical called 'sodium nitrite' kills the 'botulism bacteria', which can survive in salted meat. Sodium nitrite also colours grey meat red, which consumers tend to prefer.

HOW DOES SALT-CURING WORK?

Salt draws out moisture from food, slowing down the growth of the water-loving bacteria that feed on meat and make it rotten. How does salt do this? The cells of animals are enclosed in fine 'membranes' through which water can come and go.

When a high concentration of salt is placed outside a cell membrane, water 'molecules' leave the cell by a process called 'osmosis'. By reducing the water in meat, salt concentrates the flavour, which is why many people love salt-cured meat.

SALT IN THE ANCIENT WORLD

The earliest humans needed salt in their diets as much as we do, and they probably followed animal trails to 'salt licks' (surface deposits of salt). The trails eventually became roads, and settlements grew beside them. But as humans shifted from hunting to farming and their salt-rich, meaty diet changed to cereals, they had to find new ways of getting the salt they needed, by harvesting it from the sea and digging it out of the ground.

CHINA

The earliest evidence of salt-making has been found at Lake Yuncheng in Shanxi province, China, dating to around 6000 BCE. People harvested salt from the surface of the lake during hot summers. Salt production flourished in ancient China – a book written in about 2700 BCE mentions over 40 different kinds of salt and describes methods of extraction. One of the first known taxes was a salt tax, raised by Emperor Hsia Yu in 2200 BCE. By 800 BCE, salt was being made by filling clay containers with seawater and boiling away the water.

According to Chinese legend, this man, Chang Dao-Ling, struck the ground with his sword and a well of saltwater appeared.

SALTY LANGUAGE

We can tell how much the Romans valued salt by the number of words that come from the Latin for salt – *sal*.
- A soldier's pay was called *salarium argentium* (salt money), because it allowed him to buy the precious stuff. From this we get the word 'salary'.
- The word 'soldier' ultimately comes from 'salt'.
- We get the word 'salad' from the fact that the Romans salted their leafy greens and vegetables.
- 'Sausage' comes from the Latin *salsus* (salted). 'Sauce' comes from the same origin.
- The Romans knew that salt was healthy as well as tasty, and named their goddess of health *Salus*, after the mineral.

THE MEDITERRANEAN

The Chinese art of salt-making eventually spread west, via nomads and traders, to the civilisations around the Mediterranean. Salt became a valuable trade item for the ancient Phoenician people and their empire. Egyptian art from 1450 BCE records salt harvesting in the Nile marshes. In ancient Greece, salt was often exchanged for slaves, giving rise to the expression 'not worth his salt'.

During the Roman Empire, slaves were sent to work in salt mines, where life expectancy was very short. But most salt production was by evaporating seawater, or brine from salt springs, which they did in large, lead-lined pans. Salt routes crisscrossed the empire. One of the oldest and busiest was the *Via Salaria* (Salt Road), which led from Rome to the Adriatic Sea.

Ancient Egyptians harvested salt at salt lakes such as this one on the Nile Delta.

DID YOU KNOW?

In ancient times, conquering armies would sometimes 'salt the earth' of sacked cities to stop crops growing and make it harder for the city to rise again.

SALT AND OUR HEALTH

Salt doesn't only make food tastier, it's also vital for our health. And it's not just humans that depend on it but also animals and some plants. As we can't produce salt ourselves, we must get it from the food we eat. We need to eat a certain amount of salt every day to replace the salt we lose when we sweat or go to the toilet. However, we should be careful not to consume too much salt. There is evidence to suggest that a high salt intake makes us vulnerable to diseases of the heart or blood vessels.

DIGESTION

The taste of salt tells your body to produce saliva and 'gastric juice' (liquid secreted by the stomach), both of which are essential for digestion. Also, the chemicals in salt – sodium and chloride – are present in saliva and gastric juice, as well as 'pancreatic juice' and 'bile' (liquids produced by the pancreas and liver), which all help in the process of breaking down food and releasing nutrients to the body.

Many scientists believe that a high salt diet can lead to high blood pressure.

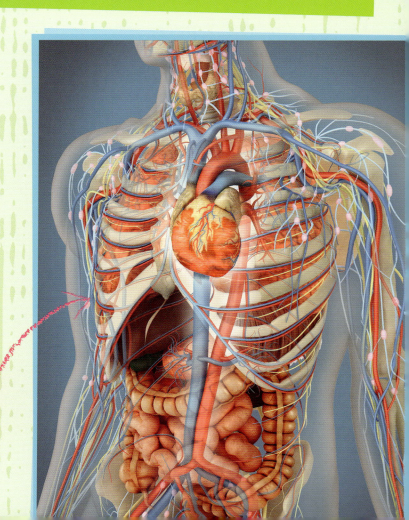

HELPING THE BODY FUNCTION

The sodium in salt helps:
- send signals to and from the muscles through the nerves
- regulate the amount of water in the body.

The chloride in salt helps:
- the blood carry 'carbon dioxide' from different parts of the body to the lungs
- control the balance of acid in the body
- the body absorb 'potassium'.

HOW MUCH SALT SHOULD WE EAT?

We don't actually need a lot of salt to remain healthy. The experts recommend:

3 g a day
4–6 year olds

5 g a day
7–10 year olds

6 g a day
11 year olds and over

Many of the foods we buy from shops, including bread, biscuits, canned foods and breakfast cereals, already have salt in them, so we don't need to add any extra. Too much salt, like too much of anything, is bad for your health.

Excessive sodium in the body is called *hypernatraemia*. This is usually caused by dehydration, but can sometimes be the result of eating too much salty food. Too little salt can also be dangerous. A lack of sodium (*hyponatraemia*) might happen if a person drinks too much water, causing the sodium in their body to become diluted.

Foods with high salt content should be eaten in moderation.

HEALTH SUPPLEMENTS

In North America, iodine is added to most salt. It was first introduced in the 1920s to reduce Iodine Deficiency Disorder (IDD). This can cause serious health problems.

Iodising salt has virtually eliminated IDD in North America. Fluoride, a mineral that helps reduce the risk of tooth decay, is also sometimes added to salt.

SALT IN RELIGION

Salt is essential to human life, so it's not surprising that it has played a major part in the world's religions. The earliest civilisations performed religious and magical rites involving salt. For many religions it was a symbol of unchanging and everlasting purity.

GREECE AND ROME

The ancient Greeks used salt during their religious rituals, for example rubbing a flat stone with brine before performing an animal sacrifice on it. In ancient Rome, the Vestal Virgins (priestesses of the goddess Vesta) used a mixture of salt and flour as part of their sacrifices. They would pour this *mola salsa* (salted flour) on the forehead and between the horns of the animal before slaughtering it. If the salt fell off, it was a sign of Vesta's displeasure. From this we get the superstition, still believed by some people today, that spilled salt is bad luck. We can recognise Judas Iscariot, the betrayer of Jesus, in the famous painting by Leonardo da Vinci, *The Last Supper*, because he has spilled some salt.

In *The Last Supper* by Leonardo da Vinci, Judas is shown spilling the salt.

BUDDHISM AND SHINTO

Salt symbolises purity in other faiths, too. In Buddhism and Shinto, salt is used to purify an area. Buddhists throw salt over their shoulder before entering their home after a funeral, to scare off evil spirits that might be clinging to their back. It is also used in sumo wrestling, which began as a Shinto rite. Before wrestlers enter the ring for a fight, salt is thrown onto the floor to drive off evil spirits.

A Buddhist monk throws salts to cleanse or purify the way before a ceremony in Japan.

JUDAISM AND CHRISTIANITY

The Jews used salt in their temple sacrifices, and still dip their bread in salt on the Sabbath to commemorate this. Jesus called his disciples 'the salt of the earth', and to this day, it describes people who are kind, reliable and honest.

Covenants in both Old and New Testaments were often sealed with salt. This was because salt preserved meat and made it clean, so it became a symbol of stability and purity. Until the 1960s, Roman Catholics placed a little salt on a baby's lip during baptism as a purifying ritual. In one Bible story, however, salt symbolised a lack of faith. In the Book of Genesis, two angels of the Lord commanded Lot, his wife and daughters to flee the sinful city of Sodom without ever looking back. When Lot's wife glanced back (because she lacked faith), she was turned into a pillar of salt.

SALTY SUPERSTITIONS

In one medieval European superstition, if someone accidentally spilled some salt, they would have to cast a pinch of it over their left shoulder. This was done to send away any evil spirits that may be gathering there, and possibly send them to someone else. The idea was that salt brought bad luck to those who spilt it, but gave bad luck to others if it was thrown. This is contradicted by another European custom in which salt is thrown into a coffin before burial to protect the dead person from the devil.

SALT IN THE MIDDLE AGES

During the Middle Ages, salt played a central role in the rise and fall of cities and kingdoms. It was traded over vast distances in Europe, Asia and North Africa. Caravans consisting of up to 40,000 camels journeyed hundreds of kilometres across the Sahara, bringing salt from the Mediterranean to the inland markets of the Sahel. Timbuktu in West Africa became rich and powerful from the salt trade.

SALT-MAKING CENTRES

The names of many cities give clues to their history as salt-making centres, including Salzburg ('salt city'), Austria; Hallstatt (from halos, Greek for 'salt'), Germany; Tuzla (tuz is Turkish for 'salt'), Bosnia-Herzegovina; and As-Salt, Jordan. In Britain, salt was harvested from salt springs. The towns that grew up around these had the suffix '-wich' ('marsh') and included Norwich, Middlewich, Nantwich and Droitwich. The salt was transported from these production centres along regular salt routes, such as Old Salt Road in northern Germany, which ran from the salt mine in Lüneburg.

Lubeck in Germany, at the northern end of the Old Salt Road.

Venice grew rich on the salt trade.

VENICE

The medieval city-state of Venice rose to prominence thanks largely to salt. From the 10th century, the Venetians set out to dominate the salt trade. First, they defeated local salt-making rivals Comacchio and Ravenna, then they used their powerful navy to force all ships carrying salt to pass through Venice. Typically, Venetian merchants would buy salt for one ducat (a gold coin) a ton, and sell it for 33 ducats a ton. The profits from such deals made the city extremely rich and powerful.

TAXES

Cities and states along the salt routes charged merchants high taxes for passing through their territory. Cities like Munich, Germany grew rich on salt-tax revenue. The African kingdom of Ghana (flourished 300–1235 CE) became a powerful empire, largely thanks to the taxes received from trans-Saharan salt traders. But the most notorious salt tax was the *gabelle* of France. First raised in the 13th century, the tax became higher and higher. Between 1630 and 1720, it increased tenfold. The government forced all citizens over the age of eight to purchase a minimum amount of salt every week at a fixed price. Anger at the gabelle was so great that it helped ignite the French Revolution in 1789. The tax was ended in 1790.

SALT MONEY

Salt was valued so highly it was often used as a currency in its own right. In parts of central Africa, cakes of salt were used as coins, and in Ethiopia they used long bars of rock salt, called *amole*, as money. The Venetian traveller Marco Polo reported in 1295 that in China tiny cakes of salt were pressed with images of the Grand Khan and used as coins.

DID YOU KNOW?

In the Middle Ages, salt was so expensive it was sometimes called 'white gold'.

EXPLORING THE NEW WORLD

Salt was being produced in the Americas for hundreds of years before the arrival of the first Europeans. In fact, the Native American name for the Caribbean island of St Martin was *Soualiga*, or Land of Salt, due to its salt pans. Early European explorers made use of the salt-harvesting skills of Native Americans to preserve and season their food.

HOW DO YOU SALT YOUR FISH?

Had it not been for salt, the history of the European settlement of North America might have been very different. When Europeans discovered the rich fishing grounds of the Grand Banks of Newfoundland at the end of the 15th century, they all began fishing there. But their ways of preserving their catch differed.

The Spanish and Portuguese salted their fish on board ship, then dried them on their return to Europe. British and French fishermen, however, preferred to salt and dry their catch on racks onshore at the end of each day. Thus it was the British and French who established the first settlements in North America, not the Spanish and Portuguese.

Fresh saltwater sardines preserved in salt.

THE 'SALT MOUNTAIN'

Salt helped drive the first European expedition into what is now the western USA. In 1803, the USA purchased the territory of Louisiana from France. Rumours spread of a vast mountain of salt near the Missouri River. President Jefferson even made a speech about it, and Meriwether Lewis and William Clark led an expedition in 1805–6.

They didn't find the salt mountain, but Lewis and Clark did make it all the way to the Pacific coast of Oregon. By this time, they had run out of salt for preserving their meat. Luckily the local Tillamook tribe showed them how to make salt by boiling sea water, and they returned with 28 gallons of 'fine, strong and white' salt.

William Clark (1770-1838), American explorer.

THE GREAT SALT LAKE

The Great Salt Lake of Utah is the largest saltwater lake in the western hemisphere and was a valuable source of salt for centuries before the Europeans arrived. In the early 1800s, explorers such as Jedediah Smith, John Fremont and Kit Carson gathered salt there. Word soon spread that the mineral could simply be scooped from the rocks on the lake shore. This encouraged the first Mormon settlers in 1847, who founded Salt Lake City near the lake. The first saltworks were built in 1848.

SALT WARS

Salt has been the cause of many wars through history. One of the earliest was a series of conflicts that occurred in the Three Gorges region of China between 770 and 476 BCE. Four kingdoms, the Ba, Chu, Shu and Qin, fought each other for control of the brine springs there, so they could make salt. The Qin ultimately proved victorious and went on to unite China under their rule.

PERUGIA AND THE PAPAL STATES

In 1540, Pope Paul III ordered the people of Perugia (an Italian city under the pope's control) to pay a new salt tax. The Perugians, who were still suffering the effects of a disastrous harvest, rebelled. But with less than 2,000 soldiers they were no match for the Papal army and were soon forced to surrender.

According to legend, the Perugians continued their protest at the papal tax in a quieter way: from 1540 they stopped putting salt in their bread. Unsalted bread remains the custom in Perugia to this day, though it's not certain that the tradition dates from that time.

NAPOLEON'S RETREAT FROM MOSCOW

The disastrous French invasion of Russia marked a turning point in the fortunes of Napoleon Bonaparte – and salt played its part in the catastrophe. Napoleon's *Grande Armée*, numbering some 680,000 soldiers, invaded in 1812, but the Russians retreated, evacuating and burning their capital, Moscow. The French army, exhausted and starving through lack of supplies, was forced to turn for home. During the journey, it had to face the freezing Russian winter, continual harassment by the enemy, and a lack of salt. Just 27,000 fit soldiers remained at the end of the long trek. Thousands may have died because they had been so weakened by the lack of salt that their wounds would not heal.

THE DUTCH REVOLT

During the 1570s, the Dutch rose up in revolt against their Spanish rulers, and a major part of their campaign involved salt. The Dutch used their powerful navy to patrol their coastlines and prevent the Spanish from exporting their salt to the cities of northern Europe. The loss of this trade ended up bankrupting Spain, despite all the gold it had imported from its American colonies – proving that, in some ways, salt was even more valuable than gold! The Dutch eventually won their independence in 1609.

A battle between the Dutch and Spanish navies in 1573, during the Dutch Revolt.

THE EL PASO SALT WAR

Starting in the late 1860s, a conflict raged over control of the salt lakes near El Paso, west Texas. The dispute was between the so-called 'Salt Ring', led (from 1872) by Charles Howard, who wanted private ownership of the lakes, and the 'Anti-Salt Ring' led by Mexican leaders Antonio Barajo and Luis Cardis, who considered the lakes to be public property. The feud turned violent on 10 October 1877, when Howard shot Cardis to death in an El Paso store. Enraged mobs of Mexicans attacked the Salt Ring supporters, and in December a group of them killed Howard. It took the US Ninth Cavalry to finally force the mobs to disperse.

The El Paso Salt War was fought for control of salt lakes at the base of the Guadalupe Mountains.

SALT IN EARLY AMERICA

The early American colonists made salt by boiling or evaporating seawater in coastal areas like Cape Cod and New York. Later, as people moved west, they were forced to find other sources. Towns like Lincoln, Nebraska, grew up around salt springs. In times of war, a key strategy was to deny the enemy access to salt.

WAR OF INDEPENDENCE

In 1777, during the American War of Independence between Britain and its American colonies, the British managed to capture the American army's salt reserves. The American soldiers were forced to start boiling seawater, but this used up too much wood, another commodity in short supply. The crisis prompted the colonists to build a chain of saltworks along the American coastline to make themselves self-sufficient in salt.

CIVIL WAR

The American Civil War was fought between the Confederacy (the southern states fighting to break away from the USA) and the Unionists (the northern states). Salt was crucial to both armies, not only for eating but also for preserving food rations, tanning leather and dyeing cloth for uniforms.

In October 1864, with the Confederate forces firmly on the retreat, the Unionists decided to press home their advantage by capturing the Confederacy's last major

A cartoon about salt during the American Civil War.

saltworks at Saltville, Virginia. But the Confederates defended well and forced the Unionists to retreat.

The Unionists attacked again in December 1864, and this time they were successful, leaving the saltworks in ruins. The Confederates had the saltworks working again in two months, but the Unionists had wrecked the local railroad system, making it hard to distribute the salt. Their attack had also greatly damaged Confederate morale. The South surrendered in April 1865.

THE DITCH THAT SALT BUILT

Ever since 1654, when brine springs were discovered there, Syracuse, New York, has been an important centre of salt production. But salt manufacturers were frustrated by the difficulties of transporting salt inland through the Appalachian Mountains, so began pressing for a canal. In 1825, the Erie Canal opened. It ran 584 km and connected the Hudson River to the Great Lakes. It required 36 locks because the land rose by 180 metres along the route. The canal was a huge success, greatly boosting sales of salt. Revenues from salt taxes ended up paying for half of the canal's construction. As a result the canal became known as 'the ditch that salt built'.

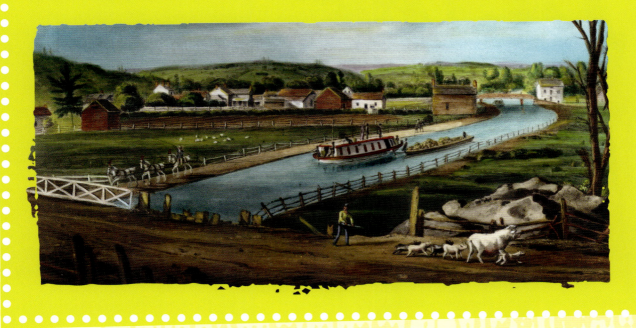

THE SALT MARCH

Salt was at the heart of one of the greatest acts of defiance in modern history. In 1858, Britain took control of India. Britain's 1882 Salt Act forbade Indians from collecting or selling salt. They were forced instead to buy it from the British who imposed a heavy salt tax. This was a particular hardship for the millions of poor people in India. Mohandas Gandhi (1869–1948), a leader of India's struggle for independence, devised a very simple yet effective way of defying the Salt Act.

SATYAGRAHA

Gandhi, known to his followers as Mahatma, or 'great-souled one', was a devout Hindu who believed that the best way of defying British rule was through non-violent civil disobedience. He called this kind of protest *satyagraha* (which literally means 'truth-force'). Gandhi decided to launch a satyagraha against the Salt Act. Explaining his decision, Gandhi said: 'Next to air and water, salt is perhaps the greatest necessity of life.'

Mahatma Gandhi on his famous Salt March in 1930.

MARCH TO DANDI

On 12 March 1930, Gandhi set out from his *ashram* (religious retreat) at Sabarmati in India with several dozen followers on a march to the sea to make salt. They walked some 390 km to the town of Dandi on the Arabian Sea coast. Along the way, Gandhi stopped to address large crowds, and every day more people joined the Salt March. By the time they reached Dandi on 5 April, Gandhi was leading a crowd of at least 100,000. At 6:30 the next morning, Gandhi walked onto the beach and picked up a lump of salty mud. Holding it aloft, he said to the crowd: 'With this, I am shaking the foundations of the British Empire.' He then boiled it in seawater, producing illegal salt.

Supporters of Gandhi break the Salt Act by making salt with seawater in Bombay, India.

NATIONWIDE PROTESTS

Gandhi's defiance sparked similar acts right across India as millions joined in with the satyagraha. The British authorities arrested more than 80,000, including Gandhi, but the protests continued. On 21 May, 2,500 marchers demonstrated outside the Dharasana Salt Works north of Bombay. British-led Indian policemen violently broke up the peaceful protest, provoking an international outcry.

VICTORY

In January 1931, Gandhi was released. He met with the British viceroy of India and agreed to call off the satyagraha only if he could join the debate in London on India's future. The conference turned out to be a disappointment. The British refused to abolish the Salt Act or make any changes. Yet by his simple action of making salt, Gandhi had shown the power of an idea. He had unleashed a force that would lead, in 1947, to the end of British rule in India.

SALT IN TODAY'S WORLD

The 19th century saw major innovations in the salt-making process. In the 1850s, salt began to be crystallised in enclosed vacuum pans. Solution mining of rock salt started in 1882. By the late 1800s, salt was being produced on a massive scale. Minerals were stripped out and chemicals added to produce a uniform product. The salt industry as we know it today was born.

THE MODERN INDUSTRY

Nowadays, salt is plentiful and cheap. Some 260–280 million tonnes are produced each year. The top producers are the USA, China and India, which between them produce 46 per cent of the world's salt. About 40 per cent of salt is made by solar evaporation of saltwater; 34 per cent comes from solution mining; and 26 per cent comes from deep-shaft mining. One of the world's largest salt mines is the Khewra Salt Mine in Pakistan, which has 19 levels, 11 of them underground, and 400 km of passages. The mine produces 385,000 tonnes of salt each year.

A monument made of salt bricks at the world's second largest salt mine in Khewra, Pakistan.

DID YOU KNOW?

In Bolivia, South America, a luxury hotel has been constructed entirely out of salt – even the furniture! Ten thousand tonnes of salt went into the creation of the luxury hotel, which boasts a sauna, steam room and, of course, saltwater baths! The hotel is perched on the edge of the biggest salt flat in the world: Salar de Uyuni. It is 10,582 square kilometres in area.

DID YOU KNOW?

Salt lowers the freezing point of water to below zero degrees Celsius. So when salt is spread over a road, it melts the snow and ice.

SALT IS FOREVER

We no longer have to explore new lands in search of salt, or fight wars over it, or go on marches, as our ancestors did. Yet echoes of salt's historic significance can be found all around us. It's in the language we speak ('rubbing salt in a wound', 'taking something with a pinch of salt') and in the names of places (like Saltcoat in Scotland or Salt River in Arizona), and it's there in the religious rituals carried out by millions each day.

Today, salt is easy to come by, yet however commonplace it has become, it will never go out of fashion. Other flavours may come and go, but we'll always love salt because our bodies need it for life. The same instinct that prompted our distant forebears to follow animal trails to salt licks still guides us today, each time we pick up a salt cellar and sprinkle those delicious white grains on our food.

DIFFERENT USES

Apart from its use in food, salt plays a role in many different industries. In fact, only 17.5 per cent of all the salt produced is used for food. Salt is spread on icy roads to make driving safer. It's also an excellent cleaning agent, used with other ingredients to clean enamel, brass and copper, or poured down sinks to get rid of grease and bad odours. Salt can be used as an antiseptic for wounds, or in mild solution as a mouthwash or to clean teeth. It can even work as a weed-killer.

TIMELINE

c. 6000 BCE	Chinese harvest salt from Lake Yuncheng in Shanxi province.
c. 3000	Phoenicians trade salt from North Africa around the Mediterranean. The Egyptians use salt in religious ceremonies.
c. 2700	In China, an early medical text discusses over 40 types of salt.
c. 2200	Chinese emperor Hsia Yu levies a salt tax, one of the first known taxes, to finance the building of the Great Wall.
c. 340	The Jordanian town of As-Salt, a major salt-making centre, is built.
500s CE	In Abyssinia, slabs of rock salt called *amoles* are used as currency.
600s	The Japanese make salt by using seaweed to make concentrated brine and then heating this in clay pots to produce salt crystals.
1000s	Native Americans make salt from salt springs.
c. 1100	City states along Europe's salt roads charge heavy taxes on salt passing through their territories.
c. 1200	In England, salt-making towns with the 'wich' suffix flourish.
1200s–1500s	Venice reaches the height of its power, based partly on its domination of the salt trade.
1259	In France, Charles of Anjou levies the infamous salt tax, the *gabelle*.
1295	Marco Polo tells the Doge of Venice about the salt currency used in China.
1550s	The spectacular Wieliczka Salt Mine, near Krakow, Poland, is opened for visits by the Polish royal family and their guests.
1590s	The Dutch blockade of Spain's saltworks leads to Spanish bankruptcy and ultimately Dutch independence.
1770	Salt making by solar evaporation begins in San Francisco Bay, California.
1777	During the American War of Independence, British general Lord Howe tries to defeat the American colonists by capturing General George Washington's salt supply.
1787–1789	Anger at the *gabelle* helps to spark the French Revolution.
1825	The Erie Canal is completed, opening up the American interior to salt producers.
1864	During the American Civil War, the capture of Saltville, Virginia, is a major blow for the Confederacy.
1877	The 'Salt War' at El Paso, Texas, reaches its climax.
1880s onwards	Refined salt is being produced on an industrial scale.
1924	Iodine is added to table salt to help fight iodine deficiency.
1930	Mahatma Gandhi leads the Salt March in protest against Britain's Salt Act.
2013	The 12th century Bochnia Salt Mine, Poland's oldest salt mine, becomes a UNESCO World Heritage site.

GLOSSARY

acid A chemical substance with a sour taste that can dissolve some metals.
alkali A chemical substance with a bitter taste that dissolves in water and reacts with acids to form salts.
anti-caking agent A substance added to powdered materials such as table salt to stop the formation of lumps.
antiseptic Describing a substance that prevents the growth of a disease-causing microorganism.
atom The basic unit of a chemical element.
bacteria A group of microorganisms, some of which can cause disease.
bankrupt Unable to pay debts.
brine Water saturated with (containing a large quantity of) salt.
carbon dioxide A gas found in the Earth's atmosphere and formed during breathing.
chemical compound A substance formed from two or more elements that are united by a chemical reaction.
commodity A raw material.
concession Something granted, usually in response to demands.
crystal A solid substance consisting of atoms or molecules that are arranged in a geometrically regular form.
dilute Make (a liquid) thinner or weaker by adding water.
dissolve (describing a solid) Become incorporated into a liquid to form a solution.
electron A particle with a negative electric charge that is found in all atoms.
evaporate Turn from liquid into gas.
membrane A tiny, thin, flexible wall that acts as a boundary or lining in an organism.
mineral A solid, inorganic (not carbon-based), natural substance.
nomad A member of a group of people who travel from place to place to find fresh pasture for their livestock.

osmosis The passing of a substance, usually water, through a membrane.
Phoenicians The people of an ancient kingdom located on the Mediterranean, in the region of modern-day Syria, Lebanon, and Israel.
residue A small amount of something that remains after the main part has gone.
rite A solemn, traditional ceremony or act.
Sahel The region of North Africa south of the Sahara Desert.
salt lick A place where animals go to lick salt from the ground.
salt pan A depression in the ground in which saltwater evaporates to leave a deposit of salt.
seasoning Salt, herbs or spices added to food to enhance the flavour.
viceroy Someone who rules a colony on behalf of a monarch.

FURTHER INFORMATION

Books
The Story of Salt by Mark Kurlansky
(PUFFIN, 2014)
The Rock We Eat: Salt by Laura Layton Strom
(CHILDREN'S PRESS, 2007)
Salty and Sugary Snacks by Adam Furgang
(ROSEN, 2011)
From Sea to Salt by Lisa Owings
(LERNER, 2015)

Websites
https://eusalt.com/salt-production
www.saltassociation.co.uk/salt-the-facts/
www.bbc.co.uk/guides/zxnppv4

INDEX

ancient Egyptians 10, 13, 30
ancient Greece 13, 16
antiseptic 29, 31

Bolivia 29
Bonaparte, Napoleon 22
brine 9, 10, 13, 16, 22, 25, 30, 31
Britain and the British 18, 20, 24, 26, 27

camel caravans 18
Canada 9
China 9, 12, 13, 22, 28, 30
cleaning with salt 29
coloured salt 6, 7

deep-shaft mining 8, 28
Dutch, the 23, 30
dyeing cloth 24

fishermen 20-21
fleur de sel 9
fluoride 15
food 4, 5, 7, 14, 15, 17, 22, 24, 29
  flavouring 4, 5, 6-7, 10, 20
  preserving 5, 10-11, 17, 20, 21, 24
France and the French 9, 19, 20, 21, 22, 30
  French Revolution 19, 30

Gandhi, Mahatma 26-27, 30
Germany 18
Ghana 19
Greece 9

health 5, 6, 7, 14-15, 22, 29, 30
herb salts 7

India 6, 26-27, 28
iodine 7, 15, 30
Italy 19, 22

Japan 17, 30

kosher salt 7

Mexico 9
Middle Ages 18-19

Native Americans 20-21, 30
New World 20-21
North Africa 18, 30
North America 15, 20-21, 23

Pakistan 28
Phoenicians 13, 30
pickling 10, 11
place names 18, 29
Poland 30
Portuguese, the 20

religion 5, 16-17, 26, 29, 30
rock salt 5, 28, 30
Romans 13, 16
Russia 22

Sahel 18
Salt Act 26, 27, 30
salt crystals 4, 6, 7, 9, 30
salt-curing 10
salt deposits 7, 8, 12
salt hotel 29
Salt Lake City 21
salt licks 12, 29, 31
salt-making centres 18-19, 30
Salt March 26-27, 30
salt money 19, 30

salt pans 13, 20, 31
salt routes 13, 18, 19, 30
  Via Salaria, Rome 13
  Old Salt Road, Germany 18
salt springs 13, 18, 22, 24, 25, 30
salt taxes 12, 19, 22, 25, 26, 30
salting roads 29
saltwater lakes 5, 7, 8, 9, 12, 13, 23
  Great Salt Lake, Utah 21
sea salt 7, 11
seas and oceans 5, 7, 8, 9, 12, 13
sodium chloride 4, 5
solar evaporation 8, 9, 28, 30, 31
solution mining 8, 9, 28, 31
Spain and the Spanish 9, 20, 23, 30
sumo wrestling 17, 31
superstitions 16, 17
sweetened salts 7

table salt 7, 30
tanning leather 24
tears 5
Timbuktu 18
trade 5, 13, 18-19, 23, 30

USA 21, 24, 25, 28, 30

Venice 19, 30

wars 5, 22-23, 24, 29
  El Paso Salt War 23
  American Civil War 24, 30
  American War of Independence 24, 30